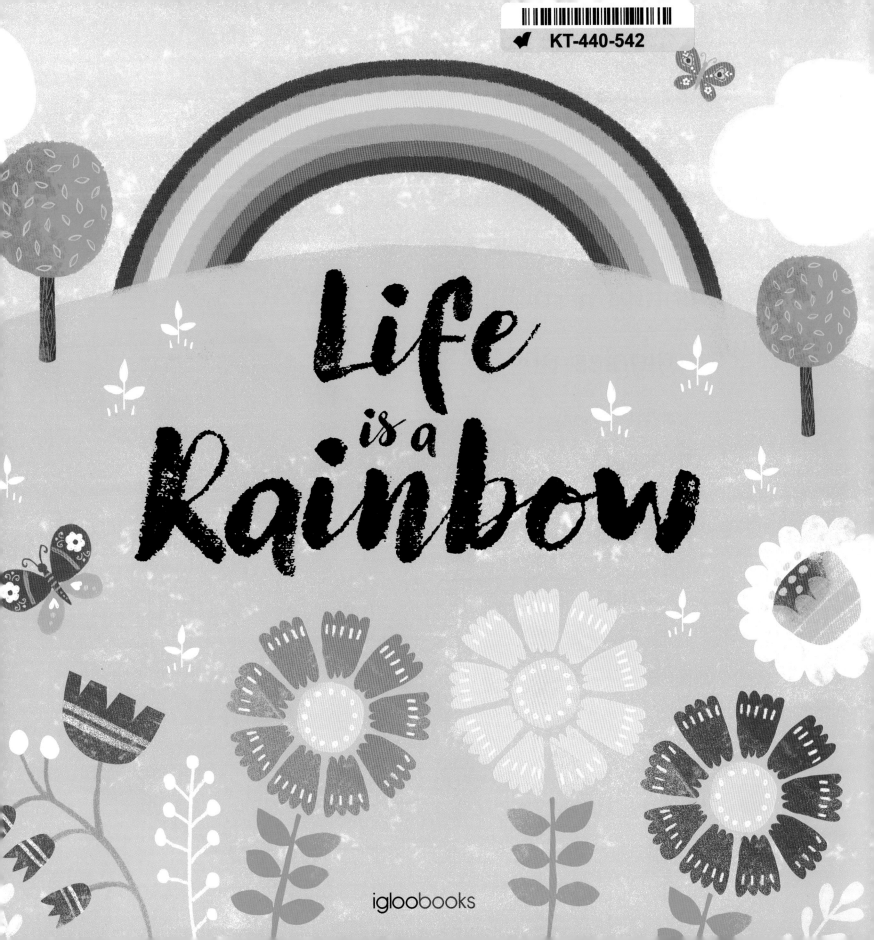

Life is a Rainbow

igloobooks

I'm painting a rainbow as bright as the sun,
with giggles and singing and hours of fun.

It shows all the colours inside of our hearts.

So, quick! Grab a paintbrush and let's make a start.

Red are my cheeks when I'm cross or upset
and someone says...

"No, you can't have dessert yet."

Red is adventurous, brave, bold and strong.

A land of excitement is where I belong!

Orange is pushing
myself in the race...

... and cheering when, finally, I win first place.

It's trying my hardest and doing my best,
even if, sometimes, I make a big mess!

Yellow feels warm on a hot summer's day.
When we're together, we tumble and play.

It's fizzy and bubbly, like lemonade pop.
On days when it's sunny, the fun never stops!

Green's how it feels when I don't want to share.

I shout, **"Give me that toy she's got over there!"**

Green is fresh air on a sunny bike ride.

Or getting a treat after helping outside.

Blue makes me calm when we swim in the sea.

The water is peaceful and still as can be.

We sit on the beach with our toes in the sand.
The clouds float above us as you squeeze my hand.

Pink is a feeling of love in my tummy,
when you make me sweet treats
that taste really yummy!

I know that you care when we pick pretty flowers...

... or you watch me twirl all around you for hours.

Purple can sometimes mean I'm feeling sad.

But you're always there, so it's never that bad.

It's darkness whenever I'm scared in the night...

... and knowing you'll kiss me and make it alright.

Put them together
and what do you see?
A life full of colour for
you and for me!

Why do the colours change?
Nobody knows!

Like rainbows, our feelings
will all come and go.

So, wish on the rainbows you see in the sky. Can you point them out when you spot them up high?

They're much more than colours. They're hope and joy, too. My rainbow is brighter because I love you!

HAPPINESS

HOME